Arsenal
The Greatest

Nick Callow has been covering football around the world for 25 years and has been bylined in every national newspaper. He was a founding contributor to the Arsenal official club magazine. He is the co-author of the *Little Book of Arsenal* and was behind the goal when Michael Thomas scored one of Arsenal's greatest goals – at Anfield in May 1989.

First published by Carlton Books in 2015

Carlton Books
20 Mortimer Street
London W1T 3JW

A CIP catalogue for this book is available from the British Library.

ISBN 978-1-78097-665-5

10 9 8 7 6 5 4 3 2 1

Printed in Dubai

Historical research consultant: Fred Ollier

Arsenal
The Greatest

NICK CALLOW

CARLTON
BOOKS

Patrick Vieira gets on the end of a perfectly weighted Dennis Bergkamp pass to score against Leicester City in May 2004. The goal took the invincible Gunners into a 2-1 lead and kept them on course to go the whole Premier League season unbeaten.

CONTENTS

"I am Gooner" was how Andrey Arshavin announced himself after signing. He soon displayed his sublime talents with this solo wonder goal against Blackburn Rovers in 2009.

INTRODUCTION

Arsenal's 50 greatest goals – where to start?

Ray Kennedy's header at White Hart Lane, or Charlie George's Wembley winner in '71? Mickey Thomas chipping Bruce Grobbelaar at Anfield in '89 or any one from Thierry Henry or Dennis Bergkamp?

The intention of this book is to bring those euphoric moments to life in words and pictures.

All football supporters have their favourites and at Arsenal we are lucky enough to have around 10,000 to choose from.

Left: *Arsenal marksman Thierry Henry performing an impressive knee slide following his goal in Arsenal's 3-0 win over Tottenham Hotspur in November 2002.*

To whittle the list down to a Top 50 I have made a nod to Arsenal's glorious history, but have largely focused on what I regard to be the modern era. I grew up on tales of the 1970 Fairs Cup, Kennedy's heroics at White Hart Lane and footage of George lying on his back after his cracker to seal the first Arsenal Double – and I never thought they would be surpassed. But then came along Brady, the George Graham era, Ian Wright, Alan Smith in Copenhagen and Arsene Wenger's relentless quest for skill and success.

For me, nothing can top the one a few thousand of us in the stands behind the net were lucky enough to see: Mickey Thomas scoring at Anfield on 26 May 1989. Has your favourite made this supreme selection?

Right: *Alexis Sanchez goes some way to justifying his £35 million transfer fee from Barcelona with a stunning volley against champions Manchester City in September 2014.*

Following page: *Thierry Henry looks on as Freddie Ljungberg scores in the last 10 minutes of play to secure Arsenal's 2-0 victory in the FA Cup Final in 2002.*

ARSENAL: THE GREATEST GOALS

Bastin, Sammels, Wright, Henry, Vieira, Walcott, Sanchez ... just a handful of the superstars who have taken Arsenal to League and Cup victories over the past 75 years.

Ted **Drake**

DRAKE'S SEVEN HEAVEN

Rarely are seven goals scored in one match, but for one player to score them all is something extraordinary. A few footballers have got five in the Premier League era, but no man has come close to matching Ted Drake's top-flight record.

Arsenal forward Ted Drake achieved just that at Villa Park in 1935 in front of 60,891 spectators. In doing so, he became the first and only player to score seven in a top-flight game. Drake had helped Arsenal secure the First Division title the previous season, netting 42 times, and he maintained his goalscoring form in the 1935/36 season. He scored a hat-trick before half-time at Villa Park, as he thrived off Arsenal's direct style and the regular feed of chances from Cliff Bastin. After an hour Drake had a double hat-trick. Villa did pull one back late on but, fittingly, Drake had the final say when he converted from another Bastin assist.

"Drake's main attributes were his powerful dashing runs, his great strength combined with terrific speed and a powerful shot."

Jeff Harris, author of Arsenal Who's Who

Cliff **Bastin**

TEENAGE RECORD BREAKER

When Herbert Chapman signed Cliff Bastin as a teenager in 1929, not even the great man himself would have predicted the impact the young striker would make and the records he would shatter at Arsenal.

By the age of 19, Bastin had won a league title, an FA Cup and earned himself an England cap. Bastin was deployed as a winger by Chapman, but his ability to drift inside and make runs behind opposition defences meant he became a prolific goalscorer. Against Sunderland in early February 1939 he scored his 150th league goal. It was a club record that stood for almost seven decades until Thierry Henry surpassed it on 1 February 2006. With 178 goals in 396 appearances for the Gunners, Bastin remains third in the club's all-time record goalscorers' list.

> *"Almost as soon as I could walk, I was kicking a football."*
>
> **Cliff Bastin**

Cliff Bastin signed for Arsenal aged 17 after 17 appearances for his hometown club Exeter City.

Jon **Sammels**

SAMMELS SEALS EURO GLORY

Arsenal ended a 17-year trophy drought to win a dramatic Fairs Cup Final in 1970 and secure the club's first European trophy. More great European nights would follow for Arsenal players and fans, but little to rival this one at Highbury.

Trailing 3-1 after the first leg, the Gunners had it all to do when the sides reconvened at Highbury. A 2-0 win would be enough thanks to Ray Kennedy's late header in Belgium, but Arsenal went one better. Eddie Kelly scored midway through the first half to halve the deficit before John Radford levelled the tie at 3-3 with 15 minutes remaining. Arsenal had the advantage courtesy of the away-goal rule but decided to go one better a minute later. Jon Sammels latched on to Charlie George's cross-field pass and drilled a low shot into the far corner in front of a packed North Bank. To many supporters of the time, this was their greatest ever moment as Arsenal fans.

FAIRS CUP FINAL | 28 April 1970

ARSENAL	**3**	0 Anderlecht
Kelly 25		
Radford 75		
Sammels 76		

"The experience we gained tonight will be invaluable for winning our next objective – the Football League."
Bertie Mee

George **Graham**

GRAHAM'S RIFLED VOLLEY

George Graham is possibly better known as the no-nonsense Arsenal manager who steered the team to two league titles, European, FA Cup and League Cup successes. As a player, the Scotland international was called "Stroller" after his effortless style and silky touch.

George Graham arrived at Arsenal from Chelsea in 1966 as a prolific striker and continued to demonstrate his talent in front of goal, topping the Highbury scoring charts in his first two seasons. However, manager Bertie Mee opted to play the Scot as a central midfielder in 1969 to combine his eye for goal with his creative flair. Of his 77 goals for the club, his spectacular volley against Liverpool remains one of the great Highbury strikes. George actually started the game as a substitute but made his presence felt in the second half. Jon Sammels won possession with a crunching tackle deep in Liverpool's half, Graham laid the ball back to Sammels, who lifted a return pass back to him in the area and the Scot rifled a first-time volley on his left foot past the helpless Ray Clemence and into the top corner.

George Graham is the only man to win the title with Arsenal as both a player and manager.

"*Our attackers enjoyed putting defenders under pressure and this goal was a perfect example of that. It was a magnificent volley from George.*"

Frank McLintock

FIRST DIVISION	28 November 1970		
ARSENAL		**2**	0 Liverpool
Graham 71			
Radford 82			

Peter **Storey**

NERVES OF STEEL

Peter Storey slots home his stoppage-time penalty past Gordon Banks. The midfielder was an Arsenal player for 15 years.

Farnham's finest was an excellent right-back, but Peter Storey ultimately made his name as a defensive midfielder with a tackle harder than a brickbat. And when it came to taking penalties Arsenal's England international was the coolest player on the pitch.

After 45 minutes of their FA Cup semi-final against Stoke City, Arsenal's dreams of a first ever league and Cup Double were hanging by a thread. Goals from Denis Smith and John Ritchie had given Stoke a commanding lead at Hillsborough, but Peter Storey, an unsung hero of Bertie Mee's side, almost single-handedly hauled the Gunners back into the tie. The tough-tackling midfielder gave Arsenal a lifeline with a fierce drive from the edge of the box on 47 minutes. Then, in the dying seconds of stoppage time, Arsenal were awarded a penalty after John Mahoney handled on the line. His team-mates celebrated as if they had already scored, but Storey still had the daunting task of beating England goalkeeper Gordon Banks from 12 yards. Under enormous pressure, Storey kept his composure to steer the penalty past Banks. The Gunners went on to win the replay, lift the Cup and complete the Double.

"We never knew when we were beaten; our powers of recovery during 90 minutes, and sometimes beyond, were immense."

Peter Storey

Ray Kennedy

Ray Kennedy missed just one game in all competitions in 1970–71 as Arsenal became only the second team in the 20th century to win the league and FA Cup Double.

KENNEDY CLINCHES THE TITLE AT THE LANE

Sir Stanley Matthews was a great footballer, but not such a good judge of a player: the England legend rejected a young Ray Kennedy when he was in charge of Port Vale. Kennedy would go on to win every honour in the game.

Arsenal made the four-mile trip up the Seven Sisters Road to White Hart Lane knowing victory or a goalless draw against their north London neighbours would be enough to overhaul Leeds and clinch the First Division title on the final day of the season. The Arsenal players realized the majority of the 50,000-plus crowd were Gunners and they did not want to let them down. Arsenal produced a controlled defensive performance and found a winner with three minutes to go. Pat Jennings produced an outstanding save to deny John Radford, but George Armstrong was alive to the rebound and clipped a cross towards a young Ray Kennedy whose towering header flew into the top corner. A nervy few minutes followed as Spurs poured forward in search of an equalizer, but the Gunners held on to bring the title back to Highbury for the first time in 18 years.

> "*That was the longest three minutes I have ever known ... I remember thinking that perhaps it might have been better had my header not gone in.*"
> **Ray Kennedy**

FIRST DIVISION | 3 May 1971

Tottenham Hotspur 0 **1 ARSENAL**
Kennedy 87

Charlie **George**

LIVING THE DREAM

For Charlie George, 1971 was the stuff of dreams. A boyhood Arsenal fan, George scored a spectacular winner deep into extra-time to beat Liverpool and secure the club's first ever league and Cup Double.

The outrageously talented attacking midfielder had scored key goals on the road to Wembley, but the Final was scoreless after a gruelling, hot 90 minutes. Then, in the 92nd minute, Steve Heighway squeezed a shot past Bob Wilson from a tight angle to shoot Liverpool ahead, only for Arsenal to equalize through Eddie Kelly nine minutes later. The stage was set for a hero and up stepped George. With 110 minutes on the clock, he collected a pass from John Radford with an instinctive first touch and drilled a shot past Clemence and into the corner. The celebration, as he lay on his back on the hallowed Wembley turf, is as legendary as the goal.

As well as scoring in the Final, Charlie George also found the net in the fourth, fifth and sixth rounds on Arsenal's road to FA Cup glory.

> *"Being a local lad, to score the winner in front of 100,000 people at such a great arena like Wembley – it doesn't come better than that."*
>
> *Charlie George*

FA CUP FINAL	8 May 1971		
ARSENAL		**2**	1 Liverpool
Kelly 102			*Heighway 92*
George 111			

It's possibly the greatest goal celebration in Arsenal history, but Highbury hero Charlie George later claimed he was trying to use up time by lying on his back.

FIRST DIVISION | 23 December 1978

Tottenham Hotspur 0   **5   ARSENAL**

Sunderland 1, 38, 82
Stapleton 61
Brady 65

Liam **Brady**

Liam Brady was at the height of his powers during the 1978/79 season and capped it off by being voted the PFA Player of the Year.

"LOOK AT THAT. OH, LOOK AT THAT!"

Liam Brady is possibly the most gifted player Arsenal have ever had. He had the sweetest left foot, could pass, tackle, dribble and shoot, often winning matches on his own. The Irish international would later return to the club as head of youth development.

After a year's hiatus, as Tottenham recovered from relegation, the derby was back on. It ended with Tottenham wishing they had stayed in Division Two. Inspired by Liam Brady's genius, Arsenal got off to a good start when Alan Sunderland poked beyond Mark Kendall in the first minute and the big-haired forward doubled the Gunners' advantage before half-time. Frank Stapleton added a third, heading home a Brady cross. The highlight of a dominant display came in the 65th minute, when Brady won back the ball near the edge of the area and unleashed an unstoppable shot with the outside of his left boot. Swerving into the top corner, it caused commentator John Motson to bellow: "Look at that. Oh, look at that!" Sunderland added a fifth late on, but Brady's stunning goal and performance still resonate with Arsenal fans today.

"I used to love shooting practice and often tried that shot with the outside of my foot."

Liam Brady

Alan **Sunderland**

When Alan Sunderland joined Arsenal in November 1977, he was viewed as a midfielder, but he was transformed into an England centre forward during his time with the Gunners.

THE FIVE-MINUTE FINAL WINNER

"Alan, Alan Sunderland" will forever be remembered by Arsenal supporters as the man who scored the winning goal in the 1979 FA Cup Final against Manchester United.

After such a miserable defeat in the 1978 FA Cup Final against Ipswich, an extra-determined Arsenal seemed to be cruising to victory a year later after Liam Brady inspired them to a two-goal lead with goals from Brian Talbot and Frank Stapleton. The match was under control as the game entered the final five minutes, but then, in the blink of an eye, United were level. Gordon McQueen poked home in the 86th minute before Sammy McIlroy found the corner two minutes later to complete the unlikeliest of comebacks. Arsenal looked dead on their feet with extra-time almost inevitable. Then, almost straight from kick-off, Brady glided forward, found Graham Rix on the left, who sent over a deep cross towards Alan Sunderland. The diminutive striker slid across the turf to just meet the cross with a right-foot volley and spark a memorable, delirious celebration.

FA CUP FINAL | 12 May 1979

ARSENAL	3	2	Manchester United
Talbot 12			McQueen 86
Stapleton 43			McIlroy 88
Sunderland 89			

" It's not like I go round talking about it – though I do have a big photo of the goal hanging over the fireplace!"

Alan Sunderland

Brian **Talbot**

THE MAN FOR THE BIG OCCASION

Having won the FA Cup with Ipswich in 1978 and Arsenal in 1979, Brian Talbot was clearly in the mood to achieve a remarkable personal hat-trick in 1980 when his header was enough to see off Liverpool in an epic semi-final battle.

A third successive FA Cup Final beckoned for Terry Neill's side and the holders had to do it the hard way when they were paired with league champions Liverpool in the semi-final. The sides played out a goalless draw at Hillsborough and were deadlocked again four days later at Villa Park when Alan Sunderland cancelled out David Fairclough's opener. Following another 1-1 draw at Villa Park, the tie was moved to Coventry City's Highfield Road as the teams squared up for the fourth time in 19 days. The Gunners dominated from the start and took a deserved lead in the 11th minute. It would prove, finally, to be decisive. Having scored in the 3-2 win over Manchester United in the 1979 Final, Brian Talbot once again rose to the occasion. Frank Stapleton capitalized on Ray Kennedy's slip in the Liverpool box and picked out the unmarked Talbot with a pinpoint cross from the right. The midfielder timed his run to perfection to plant a powerful header to take Arsenal back to Wembley.

"Arsenal were a good side and you always had the feeling that they raised their game for the cups."

Liverpool striker David Fairclough

Brian Talbot set a club record in the 1979/80 season, playing in 70 matches.

LEAGUE CUP | 4 March 1987

Tottenham Hotspur 1   **2 ARSENAL**
Allen 61   *Allinson 82*
                           Rocastle 90

David **Rocastle**

David Rocastle was making waves prior to the 1987 semi-final, having been voted Supporters' Player of the Year in 1986.

ROCKY KNOCKS OUT TOTTENHAM

Passion, heart and determination; three characteristics key to winning a derby. David Rocastle had them all – and then some. Despite his early death in 2001, "Rocky" left a legacy at Arsenal which lives on and his name is regularly chanted by Gunners fans.

Still relatively early in his first-team career, this was possibly Rocky's finest moment, as he finished off a dramatic semi-final that spanned three matches. Originally a two-legged tie, Tottenham won at Highbury courtesy of Clive Allen, before Arsenal hit back late on at the Lane after going 2-0 down on aggregate. Viv Anderson and Niall Quinn salvaged that night. Tottenham won the coin toss to decide the replay venue and were again singing about Wembley when Allen scored. Substitute Ian Allinson squeezed home a late equalizer before Rocastle's last-minute moment of glory. David O'Leary launched a long free-kick forward towards Quinn, Allinson picked up the loose ball and drove a hopeful cross into the area. Rocastle was quickest to the ball and his super first touch made room for him to shoot under Ray Clemence.

"We are very resilient and have that wonderful never-say-die attitude."

George Graham

Michael Thomas

Michael Thomas scored 43 career goals – including a dozen when he moved to Liverpool two-and-a-half years later – but none as important as this.

THE ULTIMATE LAST ROLL OF THE DICE

Liverpool had just won the post-Hillsborough FA Cup Final and would complete the Double if they prevented nearest rivals Arsenal winning the last game of the season by two clear goals. The title was up for grabs, and Michael Thomas took it.

Arsenal needed another goal – and quickly. The title decider was ticking towards the end of the first minute of injury time when Lee Dixon clipped the ball up the right wing. Alan Smith killed the pass and flicked it over three Liverpool defenders into space for Michael Thomas to run on to. The first touch was not of Championship-winning class, the ball bouncing off Steve Nicol and falling inadvertently but neatly back into Thomas's path. Another touch and he was into the area, the ball slowing up, defenders closing in, the goalkeeper trying desperately to make himself look larger than large. As time froze almost to a standstill, Thomas dinked the ball over Bruce Grobbelaar. In that moment the league trophy was snatched from Liverpool's grasp and handed to Arsenal.

FIRST DIVISION	26 May 1989		
Liverpool	0	**2**	**ARSENAL**
			Smith 52
			Thomas 90

"It's up for grabs now ... Thomas ... right at the end ... an unbelievable climax to the League season."
Brian Moore's match commentary

Michael Thomas made no mistake in the last minute of the last match of the season to win the title in 1989.

Anders **Limpar**

LIMPAR FROM THE HALFWAY LINE

Anders Limpar wasted no time in endearing himself to the Highbury faithful when he arrived from Cremonese in 1990. His technical ability made him an immediate fan favourite and his lob against Liverpool in 1992 was surely his finest moment in an Arsenal shirt.

Sweden international Anders Limpar displayed every aspect of his footballing genius in this match between the two fierce rivals, both desperate to win despite being out of the title race at this late stage of the season. Arsenal were dominant right from the first whistle and led through goals from David Hillier and Ian Wright. But this game will be remembered for what happened in the 40th minute. Limpar dispossessed Ian Rush inside the Arsenal half and surged forward five yards. The midfielder quickly spotted Mike Hooper off his line and executed a sumptuous chip from 40 yards, which sailed over the helpless keeper and dipped two yards under the crossbar. It was a brilliant piece of skill from the winger, who nominated the effort as his favourite Arsenal goal.

" To lob from 50 metres in such a game as Liverpool v. Arsenal – that's my Number One goal."

Anders Limpar

Anders Limpar had the best years of his career at Arsenal and in 1991 won the Guldbollen, Sweden's Player of the Year award.

PREMIER LEAGUE | 28 August 1993

ARSENAL   **2**   0 Everton
Wright 48, 78

Ian **Wright**

*Prior to Thierry
Henry's record,
Wright was the
leading goalscorer
in Arsenal's history
with 185 goals.*

THREE MAGIC TOUCHES

**Of his 185 goals for Arsenal, Ian Wright's audacious strike against
Everton stands out as the best. The forward demonstrated a wonderful
combination of technique, pace and balance in one movement and the
finish was something to behold.**

The England striker had started the season in breathtaking style, having
already netted winners against Tottenham and Sheffield Wednesday and
he continued his hot streak by opening the scoring against the Toffees
three minutes into the second half. In front of a new-look North Bank,
Wright was unstoppable and had the whole of Arsenal on its feet after
78 minutes with a sublime individual effort. It started when David
Seaman launched a long ball forward. Wright chased and his first touch
was a right-foot flick, which turned defender Matt Jackson, and he then
bamboozled the Evertonian with flick forwards before executing a third
successive first-time touch to lift the ball over a stunned Neville Southall,
who seemed set for a low shot. Breathtaking!

" *Everyone to do with the club has been
marvellous to me, and if it's goals they
want from me to show my gratitude, then
I won't rest until I've scored all I can.* "

Ian Wright

EUROPEAN CUP-WINNERS' CUP FINAL |
4 May 1994

ARSENAL   **1**   0   Parma
Smith 20

Alan Smith

ONE-NIL TO THE ARSENAL

Alan Smith scored a host of important goals for Arsenal, but only his 1989 header at Anfield comes close to rivalling this one. It capped a classic backs-to-the-wall performance from the Gunners as they secured European glory against Parma in Copenhagen.

Arsenal were huge underdogs against a star-studded Italian team containing Tomas Brolin, Faustino Asprilla and Gianfranco Zola at their peak. George Graham's side lacked the suspended Ian Wright and injured duo John Jensen and Martin Keown. Short on options, Graham stuck Smith in a rare lone striker role and he did not see much of the ball as Parma dominated and created a succession of chances. However, in the 20th minute, a moment of brilliance from Smith proved to be the difference. Having started the move, Smith latched on to an attempted overhead clearance from Lorenzo Minotti and his instant chest control allowed him to arrow a half-volley in off the post. The Gunners then saw off a deluge of Parma attacks to secure their first European trophy since the Fairs Cup in 1970.

"I remember seeing Alan bring the ball down and then hit it in off the near post and I had a feeling of disbelief ... it came out of nowhere."
Nigel Winterburn

Dennis **Bergkamp**

THE ICEMAN COMETH

Dennis Bergkamp was supreme in a pulsating draw against Leicester City, finding the net three times in an all-time classic Premier League encounter. All the goals were of the highest quality, but it was the Dutchman's third that grabbed the headlines.

So great were Bergkamp's strikes during this match that two of the Dutchman's goals were in the Top Three of *Match of the Day*'s Goal of the Month competition. He completed the 1,2,3 from a previous game against Southampton. And it was the final goal of Bergkamp's hat-trick that pips the lot. David Platt picked up the ball just inside the Leicester half and spotted Bergkamp peeling away towards the back post. The midfielder raked a long pass to the Dutchman, who expertly controlled the ball with his right foot as defender Matt Elliott pressured him. Unnerved by the Foxes man, Bergkamp then flicked it past Elliott with his left before slotting the ball into the bottom corner with his right. A world-class goal from a world-class forward.

> *"My first touch, or anyone's first touch, that's the most important thing in the game, I feel. And that first touch was important to make the move complete."*
>
> *Dennis Bergkamp*

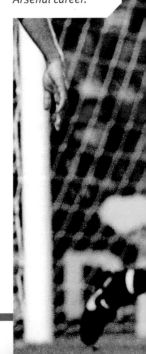

This hat-trick against Leicester City was the only one Dennis Bergkamp scored during his Arsenal career.

PREMIER LEAGUE | 27 August 1997

Leicester City   3   **3   ARSENAL**
Heskey 84   Bergkamp 9, 61, 90
Elliott 90
Walsh 90

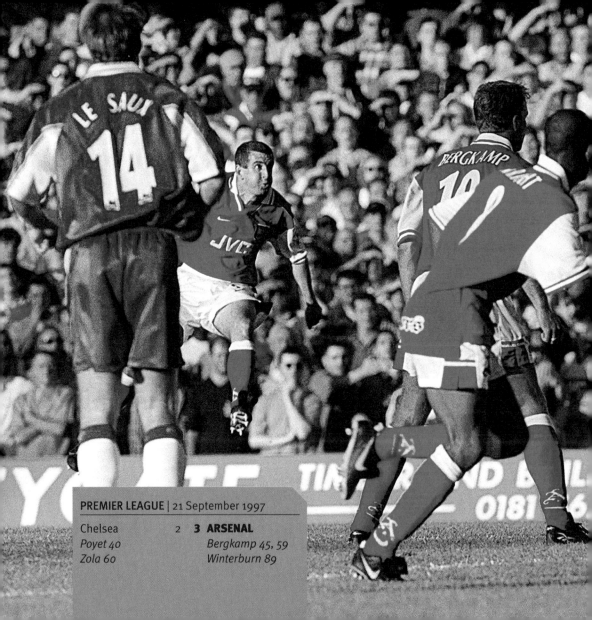

PREMIER LEAGUE | 21 September 1997

Chelsea	2	**3 ARSENAL**
Poyet 40		Bergkamp 45, 59
Zola 60		Winterburn 89

Nigel **Winterburn**

Nigel Winterburn scored 12 goals during his 13 years at Arsenal.

WINTERBURN WONDERLAND

Clashes between Arsenal and Chelsea often live up to their billing and this game at Stamford Bridge had everything. Five goals, seven bookings and a stunning strike from Nigel Winterburn, which took Arsenal to second in the table.

Dennis Bergkamp ran this early season clash that is remembered largely for Nigel Winterburn's contribution. The match had developed into a physical and enthralling affair, with Blues defender Frank Leboeuf being sent off after 67 minutes. By then the score was 2-2 and Arsenal pushed on in search of a winning goal. It came in a spectacular fashion and from a most unlikely source. Winterburn received the ball just inside the Chelsea half, driving forward towards the goal. With no one closing him down, the left back elected to let fly from 30 yards and the ball soared into the top corner past the diving Ed de Goey. An unstoppable, astonishing strike.

"I've been getting stick for not scoring for a year. The space opened up, so I thought I'd try it and see what happened."
Nigel Winterburn

Patrick Vieira

After joining Arsenal in 1996, Patrick Vieira would go on to captain the club to an unbeaten Premier League season eight years later.

VIEIRA KEEPS GUNNERS ON TITLE COURSE

There was something special about matches between Arsenal and Manchester United at Highbury during Arsene Wenger and Sir Alex Ferguson's reigns. Anything was possible when the two sides went toe to toe and Patrick Vieira's wonder goal in this encounter set the tone for years to come.

Trailing Manchester United by four points before kick-off, Arsene Wenger and his Arsenal side knew they had to win. In a defining game of Arsene Wenger's first full season in charge, Arsenal claimed a priceless three points towards the Premier League title. David Platt got the winner, but it was Patrick Vieira's goal which goes down in history. After a corner had been swung in and headed away, the ball fell to the Frenchman on the right-hand edge of the area. Running over to meet the ball, the midfielder let fly and his shot dipped and swerved as it rocketed into the net. Peter Schmeichel had been caught completely off-guard, unaware Vieira had that in his locker.

PREMIER LEAGUE	9 November 1997		
ARSENAL	**3**	2	Manchester United
Anelka 7			Sheringham 33, 41
Vieira 27			
Platt 83			

"Well, he had absolutely no right to shoot from there, never mind score."

Andy Gray's match commentary

Tony **Adams**

AND THAT SUMS IT ALL UP!

The Gunners went into the match with Everton at Highbury knowing that victory would secure them their first league title since 1991. The stage was set and in perfect fashion captain Tony Adams made it a memorable afternoon for Arsenal fans.

The first Premier League title of the Arsene Wenger era was secured and Highbury was in party mode. All that was left was to ice the cake and club captain Tony Adams did just that. Steve Bould had the ball in his own half with a minute to go, but racing past him was his defensive partner Adams. The captain was not tracked and Bould played a delightful lofted through-ball into his path. Adams duly chested the ball down before lashing home a ferocious strike with his left foot. The stadium erupted: the captain had just assured the Gunners' coronation as champions. Adams soaked it all in, walking with his arms aloft as his team-mates ran over to bask in the moment.

"Now Bould, and it's Tony Adams put through by Steve Bould, would you believe it! That sums it all up."

Martin Tyler's match commentary

Tony Adams's celebration of this goal has been immortalized by a statue outside the Arsenal stadium.

PREMIER LEAGUE | 3 May 1998

ARSENAL   **4**   o   Everton
Bilic (o.g.) 6
Overmars 28, 57
Adams 89

PREMIER LEAGUE | 23 October 1999

Chelsea   2   **3 ARSENAL**
Flo 38   Kanu 75, 83, 90
Petrescu 52

Nwankwo **Kanu**

Nwankwo Kanu made his mark for Arsenal in 1999 and was voted African Footballer of the Year for the second time in his career.

KANU BELIEVE IT?

At 2-0 up Chelsea were cruising and it looked as though the Blues were on course for victory. But with just 15 minutes to go, Nwankwo Kanu struck a stunning hat-trick to silence Stamford Bridge and send the travelling Arsenal supporters wild.

With Dennis Bergkamp out injured, there was a question as to where Arsenal's spark and creativity would come from. And those doubts were heightened when the Gunners were staring down the barrel of defeat with 15 minutes to go. However, Kanu struck twice in eight minutes as Chelsea conceded their first goals at Stamford Bridge that season. The Nigerian then completed a brilliant comeback win with a remarkable goal. After blocking Albert Ferrer's clearance, Kanu found himself in the corner of the pitch where an onrushing Ed de Goey came to meet him. Out of his box, the goalkeeper was left stranded as Kanu skipped past him and curled the ball home from the tightest of tight angles.

"This is simply extraordinary. Absolutely amazing. It's Chelsea two, Kanu three."
Martin Tyler's match commentary

Silvinho

SAMBA STRIKE STUNS CHELSEA

Two goals down and 75 minutes gone. It looked as though Arsenal were heading for defeat at Stamford Bridge unless they could produce something special. Step forward Silvinho with one of the goals of the season in the dying minutes.

A season earlier Arsenal had stunned Chelsea by coming from two behind to win 3-2, largely thanks to Nwankwo Kanu. This time, though, it was left-back Silvinho who left west London an Arsenal hero. With just four minutes of normal time remaining, Kanu drove forward and was tackled by Frank Leboeuf. However, the tackle merely rolled the ball into the path of Silvinho, who was sprinting towards the edge of the area. At top speed, the Brazilian let fly from 25 yards. The ball rifled towards the goal, swerving into the top corner and beyond Carlo Cudicini. The Chelsea goalkeeper was left in a heap by the post as Arsenal had once again come back from the brink against their London rivals.

PREMIER LEAGUE | 6 September 2000

Chelsea	2	**2 ARSENAL**
Hasselbaink 30		*Henry 76*
Zola 57		*Silvinho 86*

"What a strike! What bend on the ball!"

Andy Gray's match commentary

Thierry **Henry**

HENRY, THE EIGHTH WONDER

Arsenal faced Manchester United on the back of five successive home wins, with another victory capable of moving them level on points with their title rivals. In a tight affair, it was left to a moment of magic from Thierry Henry to separate the sides.

Thierry Henry had scored more than 20 goals for Arsenal the previous season and here he showed he was developing into a world-class forward. The transition from winger to striker seemed complete as Highbury erupted to one of the greatest goals ever seen at the ground. With the game tied at 0-0, Gilles Grimandi rolled the ball into Henry on the edge of the area. The Frenchman had his back to goal and it appeared as though nothing was on. But he flicked the ball up and on the spin volleyed the ball over a bewildered Fabian Barthez. It was a moment of sheer brilliance. It was Henry's first for nearly a month and Arsene Wenger said: "When you haven't been scoring goals, sometimes you need to try something a little bit crazy."

" You can't do anything about a goal like that. I couldn't believe it."

Sir Alex Ferguson

Thierry Henry scored nine goals against Manchester United during his time with Arsenal.

CHAMPIONS LEAGUE | 4 December 2001

ARSENAL　　　　**3**　1　Juventus

Ljungberg 21, 88　　*Taylor (o.g.) 51*

Henry 27

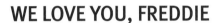

Freddie **Ljungberg**

Freddie Ljungberg would go on to score 17 goals this season, his best return in an Arsenal shirt.

WE LOVE YOU, FREDDIE

After losing their opening game of the second-round group phase to Deportivo La Coruna, Arsenal desperately needed a victory against Italian giants Juventus to keep their European dreams alive. The club's Sweden international did not disappoint.

Freddie Ljungberg finished off the move, but the Swede's strike on that Highbury night will always be remembered for Dennis Bergkamp's majestic assist. With minutes remaining, Juventus were on the hunt for an elusive equalizer – and in typical Arsenal fashion the Gunners countered. After the ball deflected off the referee and into Patrick Vieira's path, the Frenchman fed Ljungberg, who sprayed the ball out wide to Bergkamp. Juventus's defenders hurried back into shape, as Bergkamp toyed with them on the edge of the area. Turning this way and then that, the Dutchman deftly flicked a through-ball to the on-running Ljungberg. Making one of his trademark late surges, the midfielder delightfully scooped the ball over the goalkeeper and into the net to seal a memorable victory.

"I just put the ball in the net for the first goal. Then Dennis produced one of his specialities. He's brilliant at that."

Freddie Ljungberg

Dennis **Bergkamp**

In this season Arsenal collected 57 points from their final 21 games to complete the third league and Cup Double.

THE PERFECT FINISH

Dennis Bergkamp already boasted an impressive array of goals to showcase his talents, but he scored one of the Premier League's most legendary strikes at St James' Park to really cement his place among the greats. A moment of magic, which has gone down in history.

Patrick Vieira gave the ball to Bergkamp near the halfway line and the Dutchman spread the play with a pass out to the left before continuing his run forward. Cutting inside, Robert Pires managed to pick him out on the edge of the area, and with his back to goal Bergkamp flicked the ball around Nikos Dabizas with the instep of his left, pirouetted the Newcastle defender to get on the end of the touch. He opened his body up to give himself a better angle and slid the ball past Shay Given. It was one of modern football's greatest goals from an exceptional footballer. Many people questioned whether he meant it or not, but this is Highbury hero Dennis Bergkamp we are talking about here. Of course he meant it.

PREMIER LEAGUE | 2 March 2002

Newcastle United 0   **2 ARSENAL**
Bergkamp 11
Campbell 41

" Ten yards before the ball arrived I made my decision: I'm going to turn him. I knew where Dabizas was. The thought was, 'just flick the ball and see what happens'."

Dennis Bergkamp

Robert **Pires**

PIRES CHIPS TO VICTORY

Chasing league leaders Manchester United, Arsenal knew that nothing other than victory would do at Villa Park. Just as he did throughout that season, Robert Pires delivered the goods and the Gunners' title charge gathered momentum.

Brazilian Edu had put them ahead, but it was Robert Pires's second-half strike that ultimately won the match. Freddie Ljungberg picked the ball up inside his own half and played a sweeping forward ball out left towards Pires. George Boateng scampered across to close down the Frenchman, but with a flick of his right boot the ball was over the Villa defender's head and Pires was into the area and through on goal. What happened next was sublime. With Peter Schmeichel just off his line, Pires lobbed the ball over the great Dane and into the net. The winger wheeled away in delight, wagging his finger towards the jubilant travelling fans. Victory had been secured and the title race was back on.

"Well, I'm sorry, I'm applauding. That's genius. That is genius."

Andy Gray's match commentary

Robert Pires went on to be voted the Football Writers' Association Footballer of the Year for the 2001/2002 season.

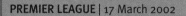

PREMIER LEAGUE | 17 March 2002

Aston Villa   1   **2 ARSENAL**
Dublin 69   *Edu 15*
                       Pires 60

FA CUP FINAL | 4 May 2002

ARSENAL **2** 0 Chelsea
Parlour 70
Ljungberg 80

Ray **Parlour**

Ray Parlour raises the roof at Millennium Stadium, Cardiff and opens up a tense game, during the 2002 FA Cup Final.

THE LONG RANGER

After being beaten by Liverpool in the 2001 Final, Arsenal were not going to let this one slip through their fingers: they were on the brink of winning the trophy at Cardiff's Millennium Stadium for the first time.

There were limited clear-cut chances in a cagey tie between the two London clubs, and very few people's money was on Ray Parlour to break the deadlock because he had scored only once before all season. But he did – and in spectacular style. Tony Adams played the ball out of defence to Sylvain Wiltord and he flicked it on to Parlour, who was the furthest Arsenal player forward at the time. He pushed on, but looked to have very few options because his team-mates were late in providing support. He knocked the ball with two touches to his right to give himself an eye of goal before unleashing a stunning right-footed strike, to which Carlo Cudicini could just extend a fingertip as it curled unstoppably into the top left-hand corner of the Chelsea keeper's net. It was only the midfielder's second goal of the season, but what a goal it was!

"It's only Ray Parlour."
Infamous on-air words from Chelsea supporter and television presenter Tim Lovejoy

Freddie Ljungberg

Ten minutes to play and Freddie Ljungberg makes it 2-0, and Arsenal lift trophy Number One of their third record-breaking Double.

THE SUPER SWEDE

Ten minutes after Ray Parlour had opened the scoring, Freddie Ljungberg put the game to bed with an equally stunning strike. It meant the Swede had become the third player to score in consecutive FA Cup finals, but more importantly it secured the Gunners the first part of their historic third Double.

Edu won the ball off Eidur Gudjohnsen around 40 yards from his own goal and passed to Ljungberg, who turned just behind the halfway line. The Swede advanced at the Chelsea backline, who were exceptionally high as they sought out an equalizer, and virtually strolled past William Gallas. John Terry's best efforts could not deny the Arsenal man, who held off the Chelsea defender's challenge to create space to shoot. Then, from the edge of the box, Arsenal's Super Swede curled an angled shot that looked like it was going well wide of Carlo Cudicini's far post before it bent perfectly into the net to seal victory for the Gunners. The Swede was the first player to score in consecutive FA Cup finals since Tottenham's Bobby Smith in 1962.

FA CUP FINAL | 4 May 2002

ARSENAL   **2**   0   Chelsea
Parlour 70
Ljungberg 80

"Freddie Ljungberg! Arsenal have now produced two absolute stunners. And this year Arsenal get their hands on the FA Cup."

Martin Tyler's match commentary

Sylvain **Wiltord**

SYLVAIN SEALS THE DOUBLE

Having just won the FA Cup, the Gunners were in high spirits. But the job was only half done. Now Arsenal headed to Old Trafford knowing a point would clinch the league title and secure a remarkable third Double.

The Gunners and United were enjoying a close rivalry as the two strongest clubs in the country, so to win it at the time was heady stuff – and to win it at the home of the reigning Premier League champions made it all the sweeter. And it was Sylvain Wiltord, making his 100th appearance for the club, who crowned the achievement with the title-winning strike. Mikael Silvestre carelessly gave the ball to Ray Parlour on the halfway line, who in turn set Wiltord away. The forward advanced and put Freddie Ljungberg in with a cleverly disguised pass. The Swede beat Laurent Blanc, who failed with his attempted tackle. Then Ljungberg sprung a shot which Fabian Barthez could only parry into the path of Wiltord, who had faithfully continued his run. The Frenchman finished into a virtually empty net and ran to the Arsenal fans behind the goal in that corner of the ground.

"WILLTORRRRRRRD!! Arsenal have scored again in the Premier League and this could be the most crucial goal of all."

Martin Tyler's match commentary

French winger Sylvain Wiltord celebrates his 100th appearance for the club with an absolute belter against Manchester United.

PREMIER LEAGUE | 8 May 2002

Manchester United 0   **1 ARSENAL**

Wiltord 55

Thierry **Henry**

THE MIDAS TOUCH

The Frenchman's forward surge from the halfway line to slot it past keeper Kasey Keller has gone down in the history books.

This goal was one of the finest scored at Highbury as Thierry Henry left countless Tottenham players trailing in his wake. The Frenchman's resulting celebration is now immortalized in bronze outside the Arsenal stadium.

It started with a long Spurs throw deep in Arsenal's half, but Patrick Vieira leapt well to clear the danger. The clearance fell to Henry, who managed to get it under control before setting off downfield with long, powerful strides. He broke into the Spurs half despite being hassled by Matthew Etherington, who couldn't keep up with the Frenchman's sheer pace. As he approached the area, the Tottenham backline was all over the place, and with one touch Henry managed to take both Stephen Carr and Ledley King out of the game before firing a lethal strike past Kasey Keller. The aforementioned celebration is just as famous as the goal: Henry wheeled away, arms spread wide, screaming with joy as he proceeded to run the length of the field to slide on his knees in front of the visiting fans.

PREMIER LEAGUE | 16 November 2002

ARSENAL **3** 0 Tottenham Hotspur
Henry 13
Ljungberg 54
Wiltord 71

"It was a special goal. It was more than important. I have never lost against Tottenham and I am so happy to say that. It's so great."

Thierry Henry

Thierry Henry wheels away in delight after slaloming his way through the Tottenham team and putting Arsenal one up in the north London derby.

Robert Pires

SUPER, SUPER ROB

Just 10 days before the two sides were due to meet in the FA Cup Final, Arsenal welcomed Southampton to Highbury for a dress rehearsal. Robert Pires was in the mood and ensured the Saints were put to the sword in a scintillating display.

This was an example of the Gunners at their flowing best under Arsene Wenger. Jermaine Pennant scored a 10-minute debut hat-trick, but it was the third of Robert Pires's three goals which stood out. Arsenal might have eased up at the start of the second half, but two minutes after the restart Pires completed his hat-trick with a sublime goal. Giovanni van Bronckhorst attempted a through-ball and Saints defender Paul Telfer deflected it into Pires's path. The Frenchman pounced on the slip and, spotting keeper Paul Jones off his line, produced a stunning first-time effortless chip from 30 yards. Pires nodded his head in delight, while the Highbury faithful erupted in appreciation of what was the start of the incredible 49-game unbeaten run.

PREMIER LEAGUE | 7 May 2003

ARSENAL	6	1 Southampton
Pires 9, 22, 47		Tessem 35
Pennant 16, 19, 26		

"We knew Robert had talent, but the Premiership has made him take on a new dimension."

Thierry Henry

Jose Antonio **Reyes**

JOSE CONQUERS ROMAN EMPIRE

Following the takeover of Chelsea by Roman Abramovich, Arsenal were not the only club making waves in London. Abramovich's big-spending team was on the rise and headed to Highbury on the hunt for silverware in this FA Cup fifth round tie.

Chelsea splashed out £121 million on new players in Abramovich's first season as owner, but it was Arsenal's big-money signing who stole the show. Jose Antonio Reyes had arrived at Arsenal in January from Sevilla, and against Chelsea he showed just why Arsene Wenger had splashed the cash. With the Gunners a goal down, Reyes picked the ball up on the right-hand side 30 yards from goal. It seemed as though nothing was on, but the 20-year-old surged forward before unleashing a thunderbolt of a strike with his left foot into the top corner. Chelsea goalkeeper Carlo Cudicini stood no chance as Reyes slammed home his first Arsenal goal in emphatic fashion. The Spaniard would then go on to score the winner in what was one of his finest hours in the famous red and white shirt.

> *"The young Spaniard has arrived at Highbury with a breathtaking goal, and that was right out of Thierry Henry's book."*

John Motson's match commentary

Jose Antonio Reyes and Wayne Rooney are the only players to have scored in their clubs' opening five Premier League games of the season.

PREMIER LEAGUE | 9 April 2004

ARSENAL   **4**   2 Liverpool
Henry 31, 50, 78   *Hyypia 5*
Pires 49   *Owen 43*

Thierry **Henry**

Thierry Henry's £10.5 million pricetag in 1999 was well earned. Eight years, and 226 goals later, the player signed to Barcelona.

THE FLYING FRENCHMAN

On his day, there was very little anyone could do to stop Thierry Henry. Pace, power and precision – the Frenchman had it all. And with this goal against Liverpool, Henry showcased all of his talents to the delight of the Highbury faithful.

Thierry Henry had already levelled the game with a very well taken goal, but it was his second that got the plaudits as he gave the Gunners the lead for the first time in the match, five minutes into the second half with a stunning solo effort. He picked the ball up deep inside the Arsenal half and headed towards the Liverpool goal with a mass of Liverpool players in front of him. He ran past Didi Hamann with embarrassing ease, and the German then tried to bring him down with a desperate lunge, but Henry was long gone. The Arsenal man was already on his way into the box, where he skipped past Jamie Carragher, leaving the England centre-back so baffled that he almost took out a team-mate; it wasn't the first, or last, time that Henry would humiliate him. Henry quickly glanced up, opened his body in trademark fashion and curled the ball right-footed past Jerzy Dudek.

"Thierry's second goal was a moment of brilliance. It was wonderful and we never looked like coming back."

Gerard Houllier

Robert **Pires**

Robert Pires and Thierry Henry linked up superbly during the Invincibles season, scoring a staggering 58 goals between them.

PIRES ON FIRE

A Roman Abramovich-fuelled Chelsea were knocking on Arsenal's door for the title, but the Gunners knew that a point would reclaim the championship from Manchester United.

Patrick Vieira's goal gave Arsenal a great start and he played a key role in the killer second too. But Pires was the conductor and the solo star of a movement, which involved 12 passes following a long goal-kick in the 35th minute. Lauren and Ashley Cole had touches, but Pires, Vieira and Dennis Bergkamp played the telling kicks in a brilliant build-up. Commentator Andy Gray called it 'a master class in football from another planet'. The move came to a climax with Pires picking the ball up in the centre circle before giving to Bergkamp, who turned and hit a perfectly weighted, first-time pass inside the Tottenham right-back to find Vieira advancing into the box. The skipper cut the ball back to Pires, who'd continued his run, and the Frenchman slotted a first-time shot. Spurs came back to level, but the point sparked incredible celebrations for a 13th Gunners title.

PREMIER LEAGUE | 25 April 2004

Tottenham Hotspur 2   **2 ARSENAL**
Redknapp 63   *Vieira 3*
Keane 90p   *Pires 35*

"We've won the championship without losing a game. We have entertained people who love just football."

Arsene Wenger

Patrick **Vieira**

THE REAL SAINT PATRICK

The Gunners were one game away from going a whole season unbeaten, a remarkable achievement for any team – but to do it in the "hardest league in the world" would be unbelievable.

Understandably the nerves might have started to kick in, for a team on the edge of greatness, and they were possibly to blame for allowing former Gunner Paul Dickov's opener for the visitors. Thierry Henry levelled before Arsenal took the lead, and who better to get the winner than Patrick Vieira? Captain Vieira, Gilberto Silva and Dennis Bergkamp exchanged passes in the middle of the park before the Dutchman decided to turn and advance towards goal. Vieira made a perfectly timed run on to a perfectly weighted Bergkamp pass, took a first touch past keeper Ian Walker and rolled the ball into the net with his second. History was made. They were the Invincibles.

"Our intention from the start of the season was to go unbeaten, because you want to win. You never know how far you can go, but this is fantastic. This team will be remembered for ever."
Patrick Vieira

Patrick Vieira made the PFA Team of the Year no fewer than six times during his Arsenal career. The last of those appearances were at the end of the 2003/04 season.

PREMIER LEAGUE | 15 May 2004

ARSENAL   **2**   1   Leicester City
Henry 47   Dickov 26
Vieira 66

Thierry **Henry**

Arsenal's victory at the Santiago Bernabeu made them the first English side to beat Real Madrid in the Spanish capital.

VA VA VOOM

"One-nil in the Bernabeu" sang the Arsenal fans as they celebrated the first English side to defeat Real Madrid at home – largely thanks to one of Thierry Henry's finest moments in an Arsenal shirt.

The Arsenal attack was relentless all game, putting pressure on Madrid, whose players looked nervy passing the ball around their backline, and were soon forced into a mistake. Sergio Ramos tried to find Ronaldo in the centre circle, but the Brazilian could not get it under control and it fell to Fabregas. He quickly gave it to Henry, who was around 50 yards from goal but had only one thing on his mind – a goal. Driving forward he rode three tackles from retreating Madrid players, including Ronaldo, before darting into the box and fending off a desperate defensive lunge, then guiding a low shot past Iker Casillas into the net. There were unbelievable scenes in Madrid and the Galacticos were stunned.

CHAMPIONS LEAGUE | 21 February 2006

Real Madrid	0	**1 ARSENAL**
		Henry 47

"It's Thierry Henry, Thierry Henry!
He is the Gunner Galactico."

Peter Drury 's match commentary

Arsenal captain Thierry Henry celebrates after giving the Gunners the lead to silence the Santiago Bernabeu with a sensational solo goal.

PREMIER LEAGUE | 30 September 2006

Charlton Athletic   1   **2 ARSENAL**
Bent 21   Van Persie 32, 50

Robin **Van Persie**

Robin Van Persie's stunning volley at the Valley was unsurprisingly voted BBC Sport's Goal of the Month for September.

VAN THE MAN

Dennis Bergkamp had left the Gunners in the summer and it was time for Robin Van Persie to step into his compatriot's boots and start a new legacy.

He started with a goal that the great striker himself would've been proud to score: a contender for "goal of the season" just six matches into the campaign. Emmanuel Eboue was set free down the right by Cesc Fabregas and whipped in a first-time cross that seemed to have missed its intended target, Thierry Henry, on the edge of the box. But then out of nowhere, Van Persie came in off the far left and leapt off the ground to meet the ball at waist height just outside the area with a lethal left foot volley into the roof of the net. Van Persie looked as emotionally stunned and jubilant as the Arsenal fans behind the goal as he leapt up to celebrate on the front of the stand.

"It was the goal of a lifetime. He's played for a long time and I'm not sure he's scored one like that." **Arsene Wenger**

Carlos **Vela**

FIRST-CLASS STRIKER

Arsene Wenger received some criticism for using the League Cup to show off his latest crop of talented players, but his youngsters did not let him down as they fired through to the quarter-finals.

But it did not get much better than this night at Highbury and one goal in particular from young Mexican Carlos Vela. The international striker scored a hat-trick of the highest order, but it was his second of the evening that got everyone's attention. Kieran Gibbs lofted a ball forward down the left, which Vela controlled on his chest despite being sandwiched between two Blades' players, managing to divert it over the deeper one in the process. He then brought it down with a good first touch, and only needed two more to take him to goal. Without changing stride he audaciously chipped Paddy Kenny with a left-footed scooped shot, leaving the keeper flapping and on his backside.

"I think he's a player who has everything in his locker of a good striker. He's agile, good first touch, very calm in front of goal, clinical and quick finisher and I just think he's top-class."

Arsene Wenger

Carlos Vela ended up with four goals during Arsenal's run to the quarter-finals of the League Cup that season.

ARSENAL   **6**   0   Sheffield United
Bendtner 31, 42
Vela 44, 49, 86
Wilshere 57

Eduardo

*Eduardo was made
Arsenal's captain
for the day, with
Wenger saying
it was "a tribute
to how well he
behaved for nine
months without
ever complaining".*

KING OF THE VOLLEY

The Gunners had already been beaten by Burnley in the League Cup, as the Lancashire side made the semi-finals, seeing off two other Premier League teams in the process.

Now it was the big one – the FA Cup– and Eduardo was back. The Croatian striker had only just returned to the side in the midweek fourth round replay against Cardiff City, following an horrific injury. He scored twice to help Arsenal past the Bluebirds, and he wasted no time in adding to his midweek brace, as if he were desperately trying to make up for lost time. Alex Song lofted a diagonal pass over the Burnley defence, to find Eduardo just onside, eight yards out. Watching the delivery like a hawk, from the boot of Song to his very own, Eduardo adjusted his stance and guided the ball into the roof of the net on the volley, with the outside of the foot he had broken 12 months earlier.

*" It was as if Eduardo was playing
football on the beach."*

Arsene Wenger

Andrey **Arshavin**

ARSHAVIN'S ACE

Andrey Arshavin arrived at Arsenal in the January transfer window of 2009 for a fee of £15 million – then a club record. On the back of this showing against Blackburn Rovers, it very much looked like money well spent by Arsene Wenger.

The Russian was surrounded by some serious hype after dazzling in a UEFA Cup-winning Zenit St Petersburg side. It seemed to be justified because he opened his account with a wonderful goal and helped Arsenal extend their unbeaten run in the league to 15 games. He had already forced Andre Ooijer into an own goal, and as he ran on to a Samir Nasri through-ball on the left, the Emirates crowd rose in anticipation. He drove into the box at pace and looked up to see just one team-mate in support. So he decided to go it alone, leaving Danny Simpson in his wake with some excellent footwork, before scooping the ball over Paul Robinson from a ludicrously tight angle.

PREMIER LEAGUE | 14 March 2009

ARSENAL	4	0	Blackburn Rovers
Ooijer 2 (o.g.)			
Arshavin 65			
Eboue 88, 90 pen			

" It took a long time to sign him, but now people can see talent is talent and his intelligence, vision and finishing is top."

Arsene Wenger

Emmanuel **Adebayor**

THE BEST OVERHEAD KICK EVER

After Spanish midfielder Marcos Senna had given Villarreal the lead, it looked as though Arsenal were in danger of suffering a first leg defeat in the Champions League Knockout Rounds that season. Thankfully Emmanuel Adebayor came to the rescue.

Since beating Roma on penalties in the previous round, the Gunners had won every game in domestic competitions, so an early goal for the home side was certainly not in Arsene Wenger's plans. Marcos Senna's wonder strike had lifted Villarreal and they were all over Arsenal in the first half. But, after half-time, things changed and Arsenal took control.

Emmanuel Adebayor could have scored with a header but could not convert Theo Walcott's cross. That was forgotten about moments later, though, as the Togolese striker executed one of football's hardest skills to the highest quality. Cesc Fabregas drilled a long diagonal ball into the box, which Adebayor controlled superbly on his chest before twisting his giant frame and hitting a stunning overhead kick past a forlorn-looking Diego Lopez. The Gunners were unfortunate not to win the game but eased to a 3-0 victory in the second-leg.

*" Today when the ball came
I said to myself 'try'."*

Emmanuel Adebayor

Emmanuel Adebayor stunned the El Madrigal crowd with a goal that demonstrated the Togolese player's flair and skill.

Cesc **Fabregas**

Cesc Fabregas became the youngest player ever to play for Arsenal when he made his debut in October 2003 against Rotherham, aged 16 years 177 days.

COOL CESC

The talk of the town was that Tottenham Hotspur were ready to challenge for dominance in north London, but Arsene Wenger's side soon silenced those whispers by putting in the type of performance that suggested the two teams were still poles apart.

A mere 11 seconds after Robin Van Persie had opened the scoring, Cesc Fabregas regained possession from the restart when Wilson Palacios sloppily gave it away; the Spaniard still had it all to do with 50 yards separating him from goal. He drove forward, escaping a wild lunge by Palacios, knocked the ball past Ledley King, who also tried to floor the Arsenal skipper, and remained calm to slot home past Heurelho Gomes. The goal turned the game on its head and put breathing space between the teams, helping Arsenal extend an unbeaten run of 20 games against their rivals. The win also took Wenger's league points total to 1,000 since his arrival in 1996.

"We gave them the ball and suddenly it was game over – we committed suicide and there was no coming back from that goal."

Tottenham Hotspur manager Harry Redknapp

Samir Nasri

Samir Nasri finished that season's Champions League campaign with an impressive record of three goals in six appearances.

A LIGHTNING BOLT FROM THE BOOT

Now over 18 months into his time at Arsenal, Samir Nasri was beginning to live up to the hype surrounding his arrival in north London. He had already found the net twice in the Champions League that season and notched his third against Porto.

Trailing 2-1 from the first leg, the Gunners needed a win to progress but would have to do it without their star and captain Cesc Fabregas. Samir Nasri was handed the reins in the centre of midfield and after making a goal-line clearance, from an effort that that would have put the Portuguese champions level, he scored a superb goal, virtually on his own, to all but settle the tie. Picking the ball up on the right deep in the Porto half, he turned away from danger and darted towards the box, shimmying past one whilst holding off another, leaving him with just one to beat before a clear sight of goal. He beat the third man with ease and drove a low shot past the keeper in at the far post. Porto were beaten and, in Nasri, Arsenal had another world-class footballer.

CHAMPIONS LEAGUE | 9 March 2010

ARSENAL   **5**   0   Porto
Bendtner 10, 25, 90
Nasri 63
Eboue 66

"It's clever from Nasri, very clever. Brilliant from Nasri. What a goal! If that sends Arsenal through to the quarter-finals, then it's a goal worthy of the prize."

Martin Tyler's match commentary

Andrey **Arshavin**

THE SUPER SUB

Pep Guardiola's Barcelona team were regarded as the best club side ever, but they were made to pay for trying to protect their 1-0 lead as Arsenal surprised them with a remarkable comeback.

Barca kicked back into gear after a Robin Van Persie equalizer, desperately trying to regain their advantage, but were soon hit by a counter-attack that would have done Guardiola himself proud. Laurent Koscielny denied a promising Lionel Messi attack on the edge of his own box before moving the ball on to Nicklas Bendtner. The Dane did well to retain possession before laying it into the path of Jack Wilshere, who played it forward to Cesc Fabregas. The Spaniard turned and set Samir Nasri away down the right with a perfectly weighted first-time, outside-of-the-foot pass. Nasri pulled the ball across the box for the on-running Arshavin, who had come on as a substitute, to guide home past a helpless Victor Valdes and send the Emirates crowd wild.

" To score against Barcelona for any player is a very crucial moment, maybe in your career ... I just took my chance. "

Andrey Arshavin

The 2010/11 season was arguably Andrey Arshavin's best in an Arsenal shirt, with the Russian contributing 17 assists and 10 goals.

PREMIER LEAGUE | 29 October 2011

Chelsea   3   **5   ARSENAL**
Lampard 14   Van Persie 36, 85, 90
Terry 45   Santos 49
Mata 80   Walcott 55

Theo **Walcott**

Theo Walcott claimed the record of being the youngest ever player to have played for England when he took on Hungary in May 2006, aged 17 years 75 days.

WALCOTT DANCES PAST CHELSEA

The 2011/12 Premier League season featured goals galore in the matches between the top sides. Unsurprisingly it was voted the greatest season in the league's 20-year history, with this match at Stamford Bridge proving to be a classic.

In one of the Premier League's modern thrillers in which Arsenal fought back despite going behind twice in the first half, captain Robin Van Persie got a hat-trick, but it was Theo Walcott who also caused London rivals Chelsea all sorts of bother as he put the Gunners ahead for the first time. His hard work deserved a goal and on 55 minutes he was rewarded. He received a quick, short Van Persie free-kick wide on the right and drove straight at the Chelsea defence. As Walcott powered toward the Chelsea goal first he was felled by a tackle from former Arsenal man Ashley Cole, but quickly got to his feet. Then, with a blistering turn of pace, Walcott danced through a bewildered John Terry and Branislav Ivanovic, before firing an unstoppable shot past Petr Cech at his near post. The Gunners had also become the first team to score five at Stamford Bridge in over a decade.

"Aaron [Ramsey] was on for a tap-in and he said if I didn't score he would've absolutely killed me."

Theo Walcott

Lukas **Podolski**

Lukas Podolski's first season at Arsenal proved to be his most prolific as the German weighed in with 16 goals in all competitions.

BACK OF THE NET

Lukas Podolski had arrived at Arsenal in the summer of 2012 and his decision to take up the Number 9 showed just what Gunners fans should expect – goals. Against Montpellier the Germany international notched his third European goal for the club with a thunderbolt.

The Gunners went into this penultimate game of the group stage, knowing that if results went their way they would make it through to the last 16 of the illustrious competition for the 13th consecutive season with a game to spare. After an uninspiring first half, the home side perked up after the break and were ahead within four minutes through Jack Wilshere. Lukas Podolski doubled the lead with a peach of a strike from his rocket of a left boot. Alex Oxlade-Chamberlain drove in from the right before being brought down on the edge of the box. As the crowd called for a foul, Podolski pounced on the loose ball to prod it back to Olivier Giroud, who fortunately was on the same wavelength. He dinked the ball first time over the visitors' defence and found Podolski, who unleashed a ferocious first-time volley that threatened to rip the net out of the ground in front of the cheering North Bank.

CHAMPIONS LEAGUE | 21 November 2012

ARSENAL	**2**	o Montpellier
Wilshere 49		
Podolski 63		

"He always does it in training. We know he has a very strong shot and he showed tonight that he is a great player."

Bacary Sagna

Theo **Walcott**

MAGICAL THEO

Going into the last game of 2012 the media were speculating over Theo Walcott's future as he waited to pen a new contract, but he made one hell of a case for a renewal in this 10-goal thriller.

Having already scored twice and set up a further two, some players might have taken a breather, but Walcott's appetite for goals was still insatiable when he controlled the ball in the corner just as the clock ticked over into stoppage time. The England forward jinked past four Newcastle defenders, ghosting between the first two before going to ground and sliding past the others after possibly being tripped. Then he used his momentum to get to his feet and chip the ball past a helpless Tim Krul for his hat-trick. The forward left the pitch to chants of "Sign him up" from the Arsenal faithful and he duly signed a new three-and-a-half-year contract two weeks later.

" It was amazing. It's hard for anyone to defend against someone with his pace. When he gets the service, he can always punish teams. In training he's no different."

Alex Oxlade-Chamberlain

The 2012/13 season was Theo Walcott's best in an Arsenal shirt as the forward broke the 20-goal mark for the first time in his career.

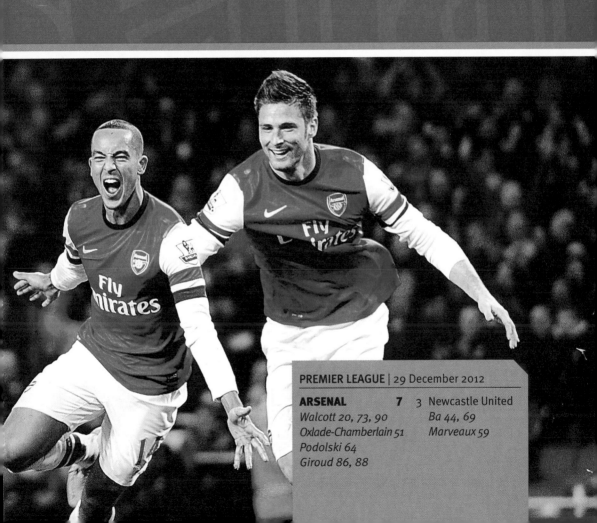

PREMIER LEAGUE | 29 December 2012

ARSENAL   **7**   3 Newcastle United
Walcott 20, 73, 90   *Ba 44, 69*
Oxlade-Chamberlain 51   *Marveaux 59*
Podolski 64
Giroud 86, 88

Jack **Wilshere**

Jack Wilshere made his first-team bow in 2008, becoming Arsenal's youngest ever league debutant at the age of 16 years and 256 days.

GOAL OF THE SEASON

Unbeaten in 11 games in all competitions since a shock opening-day defeat to Aston Villa, the Gunners were on a roll but started the game slowly after an international break.

That was until a piece of footballing artistry kicked them into gear and left the rest of the footballing world in sheer awe. Jack Wilshere picked the ball up about 20 yards from his own goal and was given the freedom of his half by the opposition. He played Kieran Gibbs in down the left, who gave it to Santi Cazorla, who in turn exploited the backtracking Norwich defence for all they were worth. A quick exchange between Wilshere and the Spaniard found Olivier Giroud on the edge of the box. He and Wilshere, who had continued his run, combined with a number of intricate flicks before the latter volleyed home one of the best team moves the sport has ever seen. It will come as no surprise, then, that the effort was voted as *Match of the Day*'s Goal of the Season.

"It was like Playstation football."

Mesut Ozil

Tomas **Rosicky**

LITTLE MOZART'S SUBLIME CHIP

There was no better sight than Arsene Wenger's side in full flow and Tomas Rosicky's goal against Sunderland was just that. A sublime team goal of swift, one-touch football that ended with a beautifully chipped finish.

After just one win in four league games, Arsenal's spell at the top of the table had come to an end. A midweek defeat by Bayern Munich demanded a response and the Arsenal did it in style. Olivier Giroud returned from injury to score two, but the real stand-out moment of this game was Rosicky's effort. It was remarkably similar to Jack Wilshere's goal just four months prior, the Czech maestro playing a part in some superb one-touch approach play before cheekily chipping former Arsenal keeper Vito Mannone. Mikel Arteta and Santi Cazorla combined to work the ball into Sunderland's half, the latter finding Wilshere, who poked it to Rosicky. Cazorla then regained possession, combining with Rosicky, who found Giroud before running on to the Frenchman's flick to dink home and give Arsenal a 3-0 lead at half-time.

PREMIER LEAGUE | 22 February 2014

ARSENAL	**4**	1	Sunderland
Giroud 5, 32			Giaccherini, 82
Rosicky 43			
Koscielny 57			

"That's what we are about, the team plays combinations around the box and it was a fantastic goal."

Mikel Arteta

Aaron **Ramsey**

WEMBLEY DELIRIUM

In the club's first FA Cup Final since winning against Manchester United in 2005, the Gunners suffered a nightmare start as Hull City scored twice in the opening eight minutes.

A stunning Santi Cazorla free-kick got Arsenal back into it and Laurent Koscielny's second-half equalizer sent the match into extra-time. Hull were tiring and Arsene Wenger's men looked to grab the game by the throat – and with 11 minutes remaining they did just that. Yaya Sanogo lost possession in the opposition area and hope seemed to be gone before Olivier Giroud latched on to the loose ball. The Frenchman produced a genius backheel to find an oncoming Aaron Ramsey, who prodded home to send the red half of Wembley into delirium. After nine years without a trophy, the Gunners were back with the silverware. Ramsey, who had missed a large chunk of the season through injury, was ultimately voted the club's Player of the Year.

Aaron Ramsey was voted Arsenal's Player of the Season for the 2013/14 season after finishing the campaign with 16 goals from midfield.

> *"It's incredible to think that I've been dreaming about this ever since I was a young boy, and to score the winner is mind-blowing."*
>
> **Aaron Ramsey**

ARSENAL **3** 2 Hull City
Cazorla 17 *Chester 3*
Koscielny 72 *Davies 9*
Ramsey 109

The goal that secured the 2014 FA Cup for Arsenal. Aaron Ramsey looks on as his extra-time winner flies past the Hull goalkeeper.

PREMIER LEAGUE | 13 September 2014

ARSENAL **2** 2 Manchester City
Wilshere 64 *Aguero 28*
Sanchez 74 *Demichelis 84*

Alexis **Sanchez**

After arriving from Barcelona for £35 million, Alexis Sanchez went on to score eight goals in his first 15 games for the Gunners.

RED HOT CHILE

After he had scored twice at the World Cup in Brazil, Arsenal splashed out £35 million for Chilean sensation Alexis Sanchez. Gunners fans thought they had secured one of the game's most talented forwards and against Manchester City their beliefs had been confirmed.

There are sometimes specific moments when players justify their transfer fee. Having arrived from Barcelona, Sanchez was already on the way to doing that with goals against Besiktas and Leicester City. However, it was during the visit of Premier League champions Manchester City that the Chilean truly marked his arrival. After the ball came out of the box, Jack Wilshere rose highest to head the ball back into the area and Sanchez's path. The ball tantalizingly looped over the head of right-back Pablo Zabaleta as Sanchez adjusted his feet in preparation. The execution was perfect. The result unstoppable. The forward caught the ball flush on the volley and it fired past Joe Hart in the Manchester City goal. Sanchez wheeled away in delight, pulling his shirt off and sliding on his knees. A new Highbury Hero was born.

"Well, what an outstanding finish that is from Alexis. It is such a hard technique to try to master."

Michael Owen's match commentary

INDEX

CREDITS

The publishers would like to thank the following sources for their kind permission to reproduce the pictures in this book.

A 2–2 draw against north London derby rivals Tottenham Hotspur in 2004 was enough to secure Arsenal's 13th league championship victory.